Illustrations by © 2017 by Liz Lemon Swindle

Published by LightHaven, 380 E 620 S Suite B, American Fork, UT 84003
801.763.7956   1.800.366.2781

He is Risen

by Liz Lemon Swindle

On the Sunday before His death, Christ came into Jerusalem and His "disciples began to rejoice and praise God with a loud voice for all the mighty works that they had seen; saying, 'Blessed be the King.' "

Luke 19:37–38

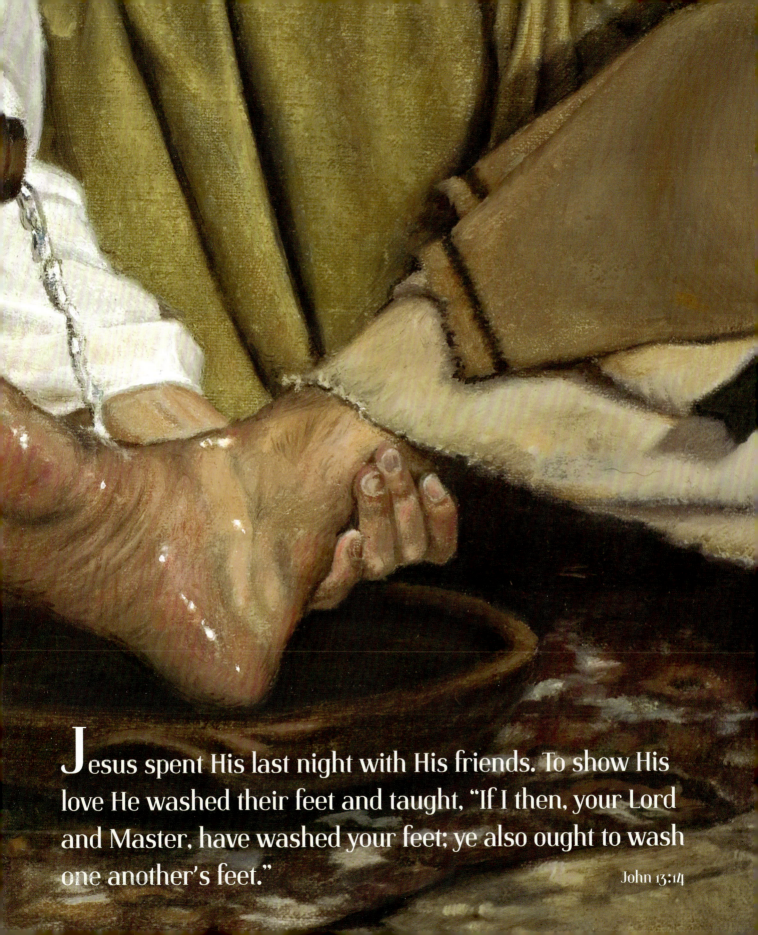

Jesus spent His last night with His friends. To show His love He washed their feet and taught, "If I then, your Lord and Master, have washed your feet; ye also ought to wash one another's feet."

John 13:14

And He took bread, and gave thanks, and brake it, and gave unto them, saying, "This is my body which is given for you: this do in remembrance of me." Likewise also the cup after supper, saying, "This cup is the new testament in my blood, which is shed for you."

Luke 22:19–20

Jesus then took a few of His friends and walked to a garden. He said, "My soul is exceeding sorrowful, even unto death: tarry ye here, and watch with me."

Matthew 26:38

Jesus felt the pains of all of us. "And He went a little further, and fell on His face, and prayed, saying, 'O my Father, if it be possible, let this cup pass from me: nevertheless not as I will, but as thou wilt.'"

Matthew 26:39

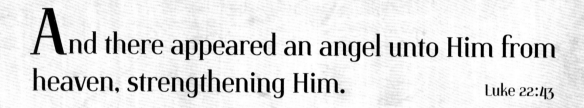

And there appeared an angel unto Him from heaven, strengthening Him.

Luke 22:43

One of Jesus' disciples betrayed Him with a kiss. "He came to Jesus, and said, 'Hail, master;' and kissed Him." Then the soldiers arrested Jesus.

Matthew 26:49

And He bearing His cross went forth into...Golgotha: where they crucified Him.

John 19:17-18

While on the cross Jesus said, "Father, into thy hands I commend my spirit." Then He died.

Luke 23:46

Jesus' friend Joseph, took the body, "wrapped it in a clean linen cloth, and laid it in his own new tomb." He rolled a big stone in front of the entrance to the tomb.   Matthew 27:59-60

Three days later Mary came to the tomb, but Jesus was not inside. Mary was sad. Then Jesus appeared to her and said, "Woman, why weepest thou?"

John 20:15

When Mary told the disciples that Jesus lived "they ran both together...to the sepulchre."

John 20:4

They found
the stone
rolled away.

Luke 24:2

*S*tooping down, and looking in, [they] saw the linen clothes lying.

John 20:5

He is not here:
for He is risen.

Matthew 28:6

For God so loved the world, that he gave his only begotten Son, that whosoever believeth in him should not perish, but have everlasting life.

For God sent not his Son into the world to condemn the world; but that the world through him might be saved.

John 3:16–17